foreword

Most people would agree that there's a place for cutlery at certain meals. At holiday dinners or fancy banquets, for instance, it might be better to pick up the ol' knife and fork instead of fingering the chateaubriand. But for laid-back lunches, simple suppers and easy appetizers, hand-held fare is a hands-down winner. Portable meals are fun to eat and they invite diners to assemble their own—a bonus for the busy cook.

That's why Company's Coming has put together this handy little book of favourite wrapped-food recipes, guaranteed to be kid-friendly, guest-worthy or both. From Grilled Chicken Fajitas, Dogs in a Blanket and Morning Burritos to Asparagus and Salmon Crepes, Nori Cones and Stuffed Grape Leaves, each dish here will have eager hands reaching for seconds and contented voices proclaiming: "Now, that's a wrap!"

Jean Paré

parmesan cones with white bean mousse

You can make the cones ahead of time and store them in an airtight container. Freshly grated Parmesan makes all the difference; the powdered variety just won't do. Add the filling just before serving to prevent the cones from becoming soggy.

Grated Parmesan cheese	3/4 cup	175 mL
Pepper	1/4 tsp.	1 mL
Canned white kidney beans, rinsed and drained	1 cup	250 mL
Basil pesto	1 tbsp.	15 mL
Lemon juice	2 tsp.	10 mL
Olive oil	2 tsp.	10 mL

Sprigs of fresh basil, for garnish

Cut two 3 1/2 inch (9 cm) diameter circles from heavy paper. Shape into cones. Tape or staple securely. Line baking sheet with parchment (not waxed) paper. Trace two 3 1/2 inch (9 cm) diameter circles, about 3 inches (7.5 cm) apart. Turn paper over. Combine cheese and pepper in small bowl. Spread about 1 tbsp. (15 mL) cheese mixture over each circle. Bake in 350°F (175°C) oven for about 5 minutes until melted and golden. Let stand for 1 minute. Transfer cheese round to plate. Immediately place 1 paper cone on cheese and roll cheese around cone. Repeat with second cheese round and cone. Let stand until cool. Wipe parchment paper to remove any crumbs. Repeat with remaining cheese mixture.

Process next 4 ingredients in blender or food processor until smooth. Spoon into small resealable freezer bag with small piece cut off 1 corner. Pipe into cones.

Garnish with basil sprigs. Serve immediately. Makes about 10 cones.

1 cone: 71 Calories; 4.1 g Total Fat (1.3 g Mono, 0.1 g Poly, 1.7 g Sat); 6 mg Cholesterol; 4 g Carbohydrate; 1 g Fibre; 5 g Protein; 161 mg Sodium

asparagus and salmon crepes

Crepes make an easy wrap for a number of fillings—just walk down any Paris street and check out the takeaway crêperie menus. This tasty mixture of salmon and asparagus makes an elegant breakfast or lunch.

CREPES

Large egg	1	1
All-purpose flour	1 cup	250 mL
Milk	1 cup	250 mL
Salt	1/8 tsp.	0.5 mL
Cooking oil	1 1/2 tsp.	7 mL

FILLING

Cooking oil	1 tbsp.	15 mL
Finely chopped onion	1/2 cup	125 mL
All-purpose flour	2 tbsp.	30 mL
Milk	1 1/2 cups	375 mL
Fresh asparagus, trimmed of tough ends and finely chopped	1 lb.	454 g
Smoked salmon, chopped	4 oz.	113 g
Salt	1/4 tsp.	1 mL
Pepper	1/8 tsp.	0.5 mL

Crepes: Whisk first 4 ingredients in medium bowl until smooth.

Heat 1/4 tsp. (1 mL) cooking oil in small frying pan on medium. Pour about 1/3 cup (75 mL) batter into pan. Immediately swirl to coat bottom, lifting and tilting pan to ensure bottom is covered. Cook for about 1 minute until top is set and brown spots appear on bottom. Turn over. Cook until brown spots appear on bottom. Transfer to plate. Repeat with remaining batter, heating more cooking oil, if necessary, to prevent sticking. Makes 6 crepes. Cover to keep warm.

Filling: Heat cooking oil in large saucepan on medium. Add onion. Cook for about 5 minutes, stirring often, until onion is softened.

Add flour. Heat and stir for 1 minute. Slowly add milk, stirring constantly. Heat and stir for 5 minutes.

Add asparagus. Heat and stir for 5 to 7 minutes until asparagus is tender-crisp and mixture is thickened. Remove from heat.

Add remaining 3 ingredients. Stir. Lay crepes flat. Spoon about 1/2 cup (125 mL) mixture along side of each crepe. Roll up. Makes 6 filled crepes.

1 filled crepe: 221 Calories; 6.6 g Total Fat (3.1 g Mono, 1.5 g Poly, 1.5 g Sat); 45 mg Cholesterol; 28 g Carbohydrate; 2 g Fibre; 12 g Protein; 364 mg Sodium

prosciutto arugula herb wraps

A dollop of crème fraîche makes a lovely garnish. To make your own, just add 3 tbsp. (50 mL) of buttermilk to 1 cup (250 mL) of whipping cream. Cover and let stand at room temperature overnight, then chill for at least eight hours before serving.

Large eggs	2	2
Milk	1 cup	250 mL
Butter, melted	1 1/2 tbsp.	25 mL
Chopped fresh basil	1 tbsp.	15 mL
Chopped fresh oregano	1 tbsp.	15 mL
Chopped fresh thyme	2 tsp.	10 mL
Salt	1/2 tsp.	2 mL
All-purpose flour	1/2 cup	125 mL
Cooking oil	1 tbsp.	15 mL
Chopped arugula leaves, lightly packed	1 1/2 cups	375 mL
Chopped prosciutto ham	2/3 cup	150 mL
Sour cream	1/3 cup	75 mL

Process first 7 ingredients in blender or food processor until combined. Transfer to medium bowl. Whisk in flour until smooth.

Heat 1/4 tsp. (1 mL) cooking oil in small frying pan on medium. Pour about 2 tbsp. (30 mL) batter into pan. Immediately swirl to coat bottom, lifting and tilting pan to ensure bottom is covered. Cook for about 1 minute until top is set and brown spots appear on bottom. Turn over. Cook until brown spots appear on bottom. Transfer to plate. Repeat with remaining batter, heating more cooking oil, if necessary, to prevent sticking.

Combine remaining 3 ingredients. Spoon about 2 tbsp. (30 mL) along centre of each wrapper. Fold sides over filling. Roll up from bottom to enclose filling. Place, seam-side down, on plate. Makes about 12 rolls.

1 roll: 101 Calories; 6.1 g Total Fat (1.8 g Mono, 0.6 g Poly, 2.5 g Sat); 49 mg Cholesterol; 6 g Carbohydrate; trace Fibre; 6 g Protein; 474 mg Sodium

deli veggie wraps

Pack these into a lunch container with a frozen juice for your kids, or set them out during intermission at a weekend sports match. If you're making a whole platter, try two different types of cold cuts for visual appeal.

Very thin deli ham slices (or roast beef or chicken), about 1/3 lb. (150 g)	6	6
Prepared mustard (optional)	2 tbsp.	30 mL
Salad dressing (or mayonnaise), optional	2 tbsp.	30 mL
Small carrot sticks	6	6
Red pepper slivers	6	6
Baby dill pickles, quartered lengthwise	2	2
Light sharp Cheddar cheese sticks	6	6

Spread ham slices with mustard and salad dressing. Layer remaining 4 ingredients, in order given, along one end of each ham slice. Roll up to enclose filling. Makes 6 wraps.

1 wrap: 152 Calories; 9.3 g Total Fat (3.2 g Mono, 0.4 g Poly, 5.0 g Sat); 34 mg Cholesterol; 3 g Carbohydrate; trace Fibre; 13 g Protein; 750 mg Sodium

nori cones

Nori are sheets of dark green, roasted seaweed. As the sheets absorb the moisture from the rice, they become soft and pliable—perfect for wrapping.

Water	1 1/3 cups	325 mL
Short-grain white rice	2/3 cup	150 mL
Rice (or white) vinegar	1 tbsp.	15 mL
Granulated sugar	2 tsp.	10 mL
Salt	1/2 tsp.	2 mL
Sake (rice wine)	1 tbsp.	15 mL
Nori (roasted seaweed) sheets	4	4
Mayonnaise	1/4 cup	60 mL
Chopped fresh dill	1 tbsp.	15 mL
Wasabi paste (Japanese horseradish)	1 1/2 tsp.	7 mL
Small red onion, thinly sliced	1/2	1/2
Smoked salmon, sliced into long strips	3 oz.	85 g
Medium English cucumber (with peel), cut into thin strips	1/4	1/4
Medium yellow pepper, cut julienne (see Tip, page 64)	1/2	1/2

Combine first 5 ingredients in medium saucepan. Bring to a boil. Reduce heat to medium-low. Cover. Simmer for 25 to 30 minutes, without stirring, until most of liquid is absorbed and rice is tender.

Add sake. Stir. Let stand until cool.

With kitchen scissors, cut nori sheets in half crosswise. Lay on cloth napkins. Using wet fork, firmly press 1/4 cup (60 mL) rice along 2/3 of each sheet, leaving 1/3 plain (photo 1).

Combine next 3 ingredients in small bowl. Spread about 1 1/2 tsp. (7 mL) mayonnaise mixture over rice on each sheet.

Layer remaining 4 ingredients, in order given, diagonally across rice on each sheet (photo 2). Dampen plain edge of nori with water. Roll up diagonally, starting with a rice corner and ending with the plain edge to form a cone (photo 3). Serve immediately. Makes 8 cones.

1 cone: 145 Calories; 6.5 g Total Fat (3.5 g Mono, 2.1 g Poly, 0.7 g Sat); 7 mg Cholesterol; 17 g Carbohydrate; trace Fibre; 4 g Protein; 276 mg Sodium

dogs in a blanket

Wrap your favourite dog—beef, chicken or even tofu—in a double blanket of cheese and cornmeal pastry. Once they're baked, they freeze well in an airtight container.

All-purpose flour	1 1/4 cups	300 mL
Yellow cornmeal	1/4 cup	60 mL
Baking powder	1 tbsp.	15 mL
Cold hard margarine (or butter), cut up	1/3 cup	75 mL
Milk	1/2 cup	125 mL
Wieners	6	6
Grated medium (or mild) Cheddar cheese	3/4 cup	175 mL

Combine first 3 ingredients in medium bowl. Cut in margarine until mixture resembles coarse crumbs. Make a well in centre.

Add milk to well. Stir until just moistened. Turn out dough onto lightly floured surface. Knead 5 or 6 times. Roll out or press into 12 inch (30 cm) square. Cut in half. Cut each half into 3 equal portions, for a total of 6 dough portions.

Place 1 wiener lengthwise along centre of 1 dough portion. Sprinkle 2 tbsp. (30 mL) cheese evenly over top. Fold both long sides over wiener. Pinch together to seal. Repeat with remaining dough portions, wieners and cheese, for a total of 6 rolls. Arrange rolls, seam-side down, on greased baking sheet. Bake in 425°F (220°C) oven for 12 to 15 minutes until golden. Makes 6 hot dogs.

1 hot dog: 398 Calories; 25.0 g Total Fat (12.6 g Mono, 2.2 g Poly, 8.8 g Sat); 35 mg Cholesterol; 30 g Carbohydrate; 1 g Fibre; 13 g Protein; 789 mg Sodium

onion apple phyllo rolls

Damp tea towels keep phyllo sheets pliable until they're baked.

Butter (or hard) margarine	2 tbsp.	30 mL
Chopped onion	2 cups	500 mL
Grated peeled cooking apple (such as McIntosh)	1 cup	250 mL
Lean ground chicken	1/2 lb.	225 g
Grated Gruyère cheese	2/3 cup	150 mL
Chopped fresh thyme (or 1/2 tsp.,2 mL, dried)	2 tsp.	10 mL
Salt	1/2 tsp.	2 mL
Pepper	1/4 tsp.	1 mL
Phyllo pastry sheets, thawed according to package directions	6	6
Butter (or hard margarine), melted	1/3 cup	75 mL

Melt first amount of butter in large frying pan on medium. Add onion. Cook for 5 to 10 minutes, stirring often, until softened.

Add apple. Stir. Reduce heat to medium-low. Cook for about 20 minutes, stirring occasionally, until onion is very soft and golden.

Transfer to medium bowl. Let stand for 10 minutes.

Add next 5 ingredients. Mix well.

Lay pastry sheets on top of each other. Cut sheets in half crosswise, for a total of 12 sheets. Place 1 sheet on work surface with long side closest to you. Keep remaining sheets covered with damp towel to prevent drying.

Brush sheet lightly with melted butter. Cut in half crosswise, for a total of 24 sheets. Place about 1 tbsp. (15 mL) chicken mixture about 1 inch (2.5 cm) from bottom edge of sheet. Fold bottom edge of sheet over chicken mixture. Fold sides over chicken mixture. Roll up from bottom to enclose filling. Place, seam-side down, on greased baking sheet. Cover with separate damp towel. Repeat with remaining pastry sheets and chicken mixture. Brush tops of rolls with any remaining melted butter. Bake in 400°F (205°C) oven for about 15 minutes until pastry is golden, chicken is no longer pink and internal temperature reaches 175°F (80°C). Makes 24 rolls.

1 roll: 82 Calories; 5.9 g Total Fat (1.3 g Mono, 0.2 g Poly, 2.7 g Sat); 12 mg Cholesterol; 4 g Carbohydrate; trace Fibre; 3 g Protein; 111 mg Sodium

greek cheese pastries

*These freeze well before or after baking. To bake them from the freezer,
pop them into a 375°F (190°C) oven for 20 to 25 minutes until golden.*

Garlic herb cream cheese	4 oz.	125 g
Large eggs, fork-beaten	2	2
Goat's milk feta cheese, crumbled	1 1/4 cups	300 mL
Finely grated Greek Myzithra cheese	1 cup	250 mL
Chopped sun-dried tomatoes, softened in boiling water for 10 minutes before chopping	1/3 cup	75 mL
Chopped fresh parsley (or 1 tsp., 5 mL, flakes)	1 1/2 tbsp.	25 mL
Chopped fresh oregano (or 1/4 tsp., 1 mL, dried)	1 tsp.	5 mL
Chopped black olives (optional)	3 tbsp.	50 mL
Hard margarine (or butter), melted	3 tbsp.	50 mL
Olive (or cooking) oil	3 tbsp.	50 mL
Phyllo pastry sheets, thawed according to package directions	12	12

Mash cream cheese with fork in medium bowl until smooth. Add next 7 ingredients. Stir.

Combine melted margarine and olive oil in small bowl. Lay 1 pastry sheet vertically on work surface. Cover remaining sheets with damp tea towel to prevent drying. Brush pastry sheet lightly with margarine mixture. Fold sheet lengthwise into thirds. Place 3 tbsp. (50 mL) filling in centre at end. Fold 1 corner diagonally over filling towards straight edge to form triangle. Continue folding back and forth in same fashion, enclosing filling. Arrange, seam-side down, on ungreased baking sheet. Repeat with remaining sheets and filling. Brush tops with any remaining margarine mixture. Bake in 375°F (190°C) oven for about 15 minutes until golden and flaky. Makes 12 cheese pastries.

*1 cheese pastry: 245 Calories;
18.2 g Total Fat (7.4 g Mono, 1.7 g Poly,
8.1 g Sat); 73 mg Cholesterol;
13 g Carbohydrate; 0 g Fibre; 8 g Protein;
541 mg Sodium*

shrimp mango summer rolls

Rice paper wrappers need to be softened in hot water. Work with one sheet at a time, submerging it until it's just softened. And if you can't find fresh mango, a can of drained mango will work too.

Rice vermicelli	2 oz.	57 g
Chopped fresh mint leaves	2 tbsp.	30 mL
Lime juice	2 tbsp.	30 mL
Sweet chili sauce	2 tbsp.	30 mL
Fish sauce	2 tsp.	10 mL
Rice paper rounds (6 inch, 15 cm, diameter)	6	6
Fresh cilantro leaves	12	12
Cooked medium shrimp (peeled and deveined), halved lengthwise	6	6
Mango slices (1/8 inch, 3 mm, thick)	6	6

Sweet chili sauce, for dipping (optional)

Put vermicelli into medium heatproof bowl. Add boiling water to cover. Let stand until just tender. Drain. Rinse with cold water. Drain well. Add next 4 ingredients. Toss well.

Pour hot water into large pie plate until half full. Soak 1 rice paper round until just softened. Transfer to tea towel to drain, being careful not to rip rounds when removing from water. Arrange on work surface. Place 2 cilantro leaves along centre of each rice paper round. Arrange 2 shrimp halves over top. Cover with mango slice. Spoon about 3 tbsp. (50 mL) vermicelli mixture over top. Fold sides over filling. Roll up tightly from bottom to enclose. Repeat with remaining rice paper rounds, cilantro leaves, shrimp halves and mango slices.

Serve with sweet chili sauce. Makes 6 rolls.

1 roll: 104 Calories; 0.2 g Total Fat (trace Mono, trace Poly, 0.1 g Sat); 11 mg Cholesterol; 22 g Carbohydrate; trace Fibre; 3 g Protein; 525 mg Sodium

crunchy thai wraps

Made from rice flour, rice paper rounds keep for a long time. Their paper thinness allows the hues of vibrant vegetables to peek through and hint at the crunchy goodness inside. Garnish with snow peas and shoestring carrots.

Cooking oil	2 tbsp.	30 mL
Smooth peanut butter	2 tbsp.	30 mL
Lime juice	4 tsp.	20 mL
Garlic clove, minced	1	1
Dried crushed chilies	1/2 tsp.	2 mL
Granulated sugar	1/2 tsp.	2 mL
Boneless, skinless chicken breast halves	1/2 lb.	225 g
Fresh bean sprouts	2/3 cup	150 mL
Shredded lettuce, lightly packed	2/3 cup	150 mL
Grated carrot	1/2 cup	125 mL
Green onions, sliced	2	2
Rice paper rounds (9 inch, 22 cm, diameter)	4	4
Thai peanut sauce	1/4 cup	60 mL

Preheat electric grill for 5 minutes or gas barbecue to medium. Combine first 6 ingredients in small bowl. Transfer half of peanut butter mixture to separate small bowl.

Slash each chicken breast half in 2 places. Place on greased grill. Brush both sides of chicken with peanut butter mixture from 1 bowl. Close lid. Cook for 8 to 10 minutes per side until no longer pink inside and internal temperature reaches 170°F (77°C). Transfer to cutting board. Slice crosswise into very thin slices. Place in medium bowl. Pour remaining peanut butter mixture over top. Toss gently.

Add next 4 ingredients. Toss gently.

Pour hot water into large pie plate until half full. Soak 1 rice paper round until just softened. Transfer to tea towel to drain, being careful not to rip rounds when removing from water. Arrange on work surface. Spoon chicken mixture across bottom 1/3 of rice paper rounds. Drizzle peanut sauce over chicken mixture. Fold sides over filling. Roll up tightly from bottom to enclose. Repeat with remaining rice paper rounds, chicken mixture and peanut sauce. Makes 4 wraps.

1 wrap: 259 Calories; 14.9 g Total Fat (4.2 g Mono, 2.2 g Poly, 2.2 g Sat); 33 mg Cholesterol; 16 g Carbohydrate; 2 g Fibre; 18 g Protein; 479 mg Sodium

chicken rice rolls

The earthy flavour of fresh cilantro pairs well with chili pepper's bite, which is why this duo shows up frequently in Southeast Asian cooking. Add a few cilantro sprigs and mango slices as garnish.

Cooking oil	1 tbsp.	15 mL
Ground chicken	1 1/2 lbs.	680 g
Finely chopped red onion	1/2 cup	125 mL
Lime juice	1/4 cup	60 mL
Sweet (or regular) chili sauce	1/4 cup	60 mL
Fish sauce	2 tbsp.	30 mL
Oyster sauce	2 tbsp.	30 mL
Garlic cloves, minced (or 1 tsp., 5 mL, powder)	4	4
Chopped fresh cilantro (or parsley)	2 tbsp.	30 mL
Chopped fresh mint leaves (or 1 1/2 tsp., 7 mL, dried)	2 tbsp.	30 mL
Rice paper rounds (6 inch, 15 cm, diameter)	16	16

Heat cooking oil in large frying pan on medium-high. Add chicken. Scramble-fry for 7 to 10 minutes until chicken is no longer pink and lightly browned.

Add next 6 ingredients. Heat and stir for about 3 minutes until liquid is evaporated.

Add cilantro and mint. Stir. Cool.

Pour hot water into large pie plate until half full. Soak 1 rice paper round until just softened. Transfer to tea towel to drain, being careful not to rip rounds when removing from water. Arrange on work surface. Spoon chicken mixture along centre of rice paper rounds, leaving 1 inch (2.5 cm) edge at both ends. Fold sides over filling. Roll up tightly from bottom to enclose. Repeat with remaining rice paper rounds and chicken mixture. Makes 16 rice rolls.

1 rice roll: 90 Calories; 2.3 g Total Fat (0.9 g Mono, 0.6 g Poly, 0.4 g Sat); 30 mg Cholesterol; 7 g Carbohydrate; trace Fibre; 10 g Protein; 385 mg Sodium

fresh veggie rice wraps

Aren't these tempting? To stop your hands from turning beet red, wear rubber gloves while grating the beets. Mint sprigs make a fresh garnish.

Rice paper rounds (9 inch, 22 cm, diameter)	12	12
Medium carrots, cut julienne (see Tip, page 64)	2	2
Pea sprouts	1 1/4 cups	300 mL
Baby spinach leaves, lightly packed	1 1/4 cups	300 mL
Grated fresh beets	1/2 cup	125 mL
Coarsely chopped fresh mint leaves	1/4 cup	60 mL
Coarsely chopped fresh cilantro (or parsley)	1/4 cup	60 mL
Thinly sliced yellow pepper	1 1/3 cups	325 mL
PEANUT SAUCE		
Crunchy peanut butter	1/2 cup	125 mL
Hot water	6 tbsp.	100 mL
Chili sauce	2 tbsp.	30 mL
Lime juice	2 tbsp.	30 mL
Soy sauce	1 tbsp.	15 mL
Chili paste (sambel oelek)	1 tsp.	5 mL
Sesame oil (for flavour)	1 tsp.	5 mL

Pour hot water into large pie plate until half full. Soak 1 rice paper round until just softened. Transfer to tea towel to drain, being careful not to rip rounds when removing from water (photo 1). Arrange on work surface.

Layer next 7 ingredients, in order given, along centre top half of each round (photo 2). Fold bottom edge over vegetables. Fold 1 side over filling (photo 3). Roll up to enclose, leaving other side open. Repeat with remaining rice paper rounds and vegetables.

Peanut Sauce: Whisk all 7 ingredients in small bowl until smooth. Makes about 1 cup (250 mL) sauce. Serve with wraps. Makes 12 wraps.

1 wrap with 1 1/2 tbsp. (25 mL) sauce: 136 Calories; 6.3 g Total Fat (2.9 g Mono, 1.9 g Poly, 1.2 g Sat); 0 mg Cholesterol; 18 g Carbohydrate; 1 g Fibre; 5 g Protein; 162 mg Sodium

spring rolls

Larger grocery stores sell spring roll wrappers, also called egg roll wrappers.

Sesame (or cooking) oil	2 tsp.	10 mL
Chopped fresh white mushrooms	1 1/2 cups	375 mL
Lean ground chicken	1/2 lb.	225 g
Granulated sugar	1 tsp.	5 mL
Ground ginger	1 tsp.	5 mL
Salt	1 tsp.	5 mL
Garlic powder	1/4 tsp.	1 mL
Chopped fresh bean sprouts	3 cups	750 mL
Grated carrot	1/2 cup	125 mL
Green onions, thinly sliced	4	4
Oyster sauce	2 tbsp.	30 mL
Dry sherry	1 tbsp.	15 mL
Spring roll wrappers	25	25
Cooking oil, for deep-frying		

Heat sesame oil in large frying pan on medium. Add mushrooms and chicken. Scramble-fry for 5 to 10 minutes until chicken is no longer pink and liquid is evaporated.

Add next 4 ingredients. Stir.

Add next 3 ingredients. Stir-fry on medium-high for about 5 minutes until liquid is evaporated. Add oyster sauce and sherry. Stir-fry for 1 minute.

Spoon about 2 tbsp. (30 mL) chicken mixture near bottom right corner of each wrapper (diagram 1). Fold corner up and over filling (diagram 2). Fold in sides (diagram 3). Dampen edges with water. Roll to opposite corner and press to seal (diagram 4).

Deep-fry, in batches, in hot (375°F, 190°C) cooking oil (see Tip, page 64) for about 5 minutes until golden. Transfer to paper towels to drain. Makes 25 spring rolls.

1 spring roll: 85 Calories; 1.9 g Total Fat (0.9 g Mono, 0.5 g Poly, 0.2 g Sat); 8 mg Cholesterol; 12 g Carbohydrate; 1 g Fibre; 4 g Protein; 336 mg Sodium

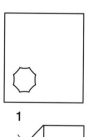

1

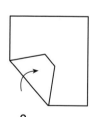

2

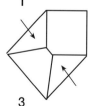

3

4

crispy jerk chicken rolls

Buy ready-made jerk paste or design your own by playing with onion salt or flakes, thyme, cinnamon, cloves, allspice, cayenne, fresh ginger and garlic until you like the taste. To wrap up these flavour sensations, follow the diagrams on page 26.

Cooking oil	1 tsp.	5 mL
Chopped onion	1 cup	250 mL
Grated carrot	1 cup	250 mL
Chopped pickled jalapeño pepper	1 tbsp.	15 mL
Jerk paste	1 1/4 tsp.	6 mL
Garlic clove, minced	1	1
Ground allspice	1/8 tsp.	0.5 mL
Chopped cooked chicken	1 cup	250 mL
Plain yogurt	2 tbsp.	30 mL
Spring roll wrappers (6 inch, 15 cm, square)	8	8
Egg white (large)	1	1
Water	1 tbsp.	15 mL
Cooking oil	3 cups	750 mL

Heat first amount of cooking oil in large frying pan on medium. Add next 6 ingredients. Cook, stirring often, for about 10 minutes until onion is softened.

Add chicken and yogurt. Stir.

Arrange wrappers on work surface. Combine egg white and water in small cup. Place about 1/4 cup (60 mL) chicken mixture near bottom right corner of each wrapper. Fold corner up and over filling. Fold in sides. Dampen edges with egg white mixture. Roll up to opposite corner. Press to seal.

Heat second amount of cooking oil in large frying pan on medium-high (see Tip, page 64). Shallow-fry 2 or 3 rolls at a time, turning often, until golden. Transfer to paper towels to drain. Makes 8 rolls.

1 roll: 150 Calories; 5.1 g Total Fat (2.6 g Mono, 1.3 g Poly, 0.6 g Sat); 16 mg Cholesterol; 18 g Carbohydrate; 1 g Fibre; 9 g Protein; 227 mg Sodium

morning burritos

Adults have finger food; kids love hand food. Here's a way to get them to eat the most important meal of the day. If you're worried about cholesterol, use 1 cup (250 mL) low-cholesterol egg product instead.

Butter (or hard margarine)	2 tsp.	10 mL
Chopped green onion	1/4 cup	60 mL
Large eggs, fork-beaten	4	4
Chili powder	1/4 tsp.	1 mL
Salt	1/4 tsp.	1 mL
Chopped pickled jalapeño pepper	2 tbsp.	30 mL
Grated light sharp Cheddar (or Monterey Jack) cheese	3/4 cup	175 mL
Whole-wheat flour tortillas (9 inch, 22 cm, size), warmed	4	4
Light sour cream (optional)	2 tbsp.	30 mL
Salsa (optional)	2 tbsp.	30 mL

Melt butter in large frying pan on medium. Add green onion. Cook for 30 seconds. Add eggs. Sprinkle with chili powder and salt. Cook, stirring occasionally, on medium until eggs start to set. Add jalapeño pepper. Cook until eggs are set.

Sprinkle cheese over tortillas. Spoon 1/4 of egg mixture along centre of each tortilla. Top with sour cream and salsa. Fold sides over filling. Roll up from bottom to enclose filling. Cut in half diagonally. Makes 4 burritos.

1 burrito: 220 Calories; 10.7 g Total Fat (2.5 g Mono, 1.0 g Poly, 5.1 g Sat); 228 mg Cholesterol; 22 g Carbohydrate; 2 g Fibre; 15 g Protein; 578 mg Sodium

shrimp and asparagus wraps

Experiment with different types of tortillas. Both the ingredients and the colours should be considered, and sometimes it's fun to have a variety on hand to please the eye and the taste buds.

Fresh asparagus, trimmed of tough ends (thick spears halved lengthwise)	1/2 lb.	225 g
Mayonnaise	1/3 cup	75 mL
Wasabi paste (Japanese horseradish)	2 tsp.	10 mL
Large flour (or basil pesto) tortillas (9 inches, 22 cm, diameter)	4	4
Cooked medium shrimp (peeled and deveined), halved lengthwise	1 lb.	454 g
Thinly sliced red onion	1/4 cup	60 mL

Pour water into large frying pan until about 1 inch (2.5 cm) deep. Bring to a boil. Reduce heat to medium. Add asparagus. Boil gently for about 3 minutes until tender-crisp. Transfer to large bowl of ice water. Let stand for 5 to 7 minutes until cold. Drain.

Combine mayonnaise and wasabi paste in small bowl. Spread over tortillas.

Layer asparagus, shrimp and red onion, in order given, along centre of each tortilla, leaving 2 inches (5 cm) at bottom edge. Fold bottom over filling. Roll up from bottom to enclose filling. Makes 4 wraps.

1 wrap: 408 Calories; 21.2 g Total Fat (0.3 g Mono, 0.8 g Poly, 2.4 g Sat); 179 mg Cholesterol; 24 g Carbohydrate; 1 g Fibre; 29 g Protein; 665 mg Sodium

turkey wraps

Turkey and cranberries are the stars of these lunch wraps. No cranberry sauce? Then let the turkey make a solo appearance. If there are any leftover tortillas, they're happy waiting in the freezer, stored against a wall or on top of something flat so they don't break.

Light mayonnaise	1/4 cup	60 mL
Light sour cream	1/4 cup	60 mL
Whole cranberry sauce	1/4 cup	60 mL
Whole-wheat flour tortillas (9 inch, 22 cm, diameter)	4	4
Chopped cooked turkey	1 1/4 cups	300 mL
Finely shredded iceberg lettuce, lightly packed	1 cup	250 mL
Finely chopped celery	1/2 cup	125 mL
Finely chopped green onion	1/2 cup	125 mL
Raisins	1/2 cup	125 mL
Sliced almonds, toasted (see Tip, page 64)	1/4 cup	60 mL

Combine first 3 ingredients in large bowl. Spread about 1 1/2 tbsp. (25 mL) over each tortilla, leaving 1 inch (2.5 cm) edge.

Add remaining 6 ingredients to remaining cranberry mixture. Mix well. Spoon along centre of tortillas. Fold sides over filling. Roll up from bottom to enclose filling. Makes 4 wraps.

1 wrap: 428 Calories; 13.4 g Total Fat (6.4 g Mono, 3.6 g Poly, 3.0 g Sat); 39 mg Cholesterol; 59 g Carbohydrate; / g Fibre; 22 g Protein; 472 mg Sodium

salami pineapple wraps

If anything can bust the lunch-bag blues, this is it. Sure, everyone's heard of mustard and salami, but mint, avocado and pineapple? Fabulous!

Mayonnaise	1/2 cup	125 mL
Chopped fresh mint leaves	3 tbsp.	50 mL
Dijon mustard (with whole seeds)	2 tbsp.	30 mL
Flour tortillas (9 inch, 22 cm, diameter)	8	8
Thin salami slices	24	24
Large avocados, thinly sliced	2	2
Can of pineapple slices, drained and halved	14 oz.	398 mL
Spring mix lettuce, lightly packed	2 cups	500 mL

Combine first 3 ingredients in small bowl. Spread evenly over tortillas, leaving 1 inch (2.5 cm) border.

Layer remaining 4 ingredients, in order given, down centre of each tortilla, leaving 2 inches (5 cm) at bottom. Fold bottom edge over filling. Fold over sides to enclose filling, leaving top open. Makes 8 wraps.

1 wrap: 477 Calories; 32.2 g Total Fat (9.4 g Mono, 1.8 g Poly, 5.8 g Sat); 35 mg Cholesterol; 36 g Carbohydrate; 4 g Fibre; 13 g Protein; 1100 mg Sodium

grilled chicken fajitas

First, grill the chicken, peppers and onions on the barbecue for a smoky flavour, then have everybody assemble their own fajita—now that's a time-saver! Be sure to lay the chicken thighs flat on the grill to speed up the cooking time.

Olive (or cooking) oil	2 tbsp.	30 mL
Balsamic vinegar	1 tbsp.	15 mL
Dijon mustard	1 tsp.	5 mL
Garlic clove, minced	1	1
(or 1/4 tsp., 1 mL, powder)		
Ground cumin	1 tsp.	5 mL
Cayenne pepper	1/2 tsp.	2 mL
Boneless, skinless chicken thighs	1 lb.	454 g
Large red pepper, quartered	1	1
Large yellow pepper, quartered	1	1
Medium red onion, quartered	1	1
Whole-wheat flour tortillas	4	4
(9 inch, 22 cm, diameter)		
Light sour cream	1/2 cup	125 mL
Salsa	1/2 cup	125 mL
Chopped green onion	1/4 cup	60 mL

Preheat gas barbecue to medium-high. Combine first 6 ingredients in small bowl.

Arrange next 4 ingredients on greased grill. Brush with olive oil mixture. Close lid. Cook for about 12 minutes, turning occasionally and brushing with remaining olive oil mixture, until peppers and onion are softened and internal temperature of chicken reaches 170°C (77°F). Transfer to plate. Cover with foil. Let stand for 5 minutes. Cut chicken, peppers and onion into strips. Transfer to bowl.

Arrange chicken and vegetables down centre of each tortilla. Layer remaining 3 ingredients over vegetables. Fold up bottom over filling. Fold sides to enclose filling, leaving tops open. Serves 4.

1 serving: 405 Calories; 19.3 g Total Fat (8.2 g Mono, 3.7 g Poly, 4.8 g Sat); 84 mg Cholesterol; 32 g Carbohydrate; 4 g Fibre; 27 g Protein; 481 mg Sodium

chip chicken in a wrap

Kids will love helping make these homemade chicken fingers in a tortilla "mitt." Get them to crush their favourite flavour of potato chips in a resealable plastic bag with a rolling pin or the bottom of a plastic cup.

HONEY MUSTARD SAUCE

Salad dressing (or mayonnaise)	1/2 cup	125 mL
Liquid honey	2 tbsp.	30 mL
Prepared mustard	2 tsp.	10 mL

CHIP CHICKEN

Large egg, fork-beaten	1	1
Milk	1 tbsp.	15 mL
Finely crushed potato chips	1 cup	250 mL
Yellow cornmeal	1/4 cup	60 mL
Boneless, skinless chicken breast halves, cut diagonally into 5 strips each	1 lb.	454 g

WRAP

Flour tortillas (9 inch, 22 cm, diameter)	4	4
Green leaf lettuce leaves (optional)	8	8

Honey Mustard Sauce: Combine first 3 ingredients in small bowl. Makes about 2/3 cup (150 mL) sauce. Set aside.

Chip Chicken: Combine egg and milk in medium bowl.

Combine crushed chips and cornmeal in shallow medium dish.

Dip chicken strips into egg mixture. Press both sides of strips into chip mixture until coated. Arrange chicken strips on greased baking sheet with sides. Bake in 400°F (205°C) oven for 15 to 20 minutes until chicken is no longer pink inside.

Wrap: Spread about 2 1/2 tbsp. (37 mL) sauce over each tortilla, almost to edge. Place 2 lettuce leaves over sauce. Arrange 3 to 4 chicken strips over lettuce across centre of each tortilla. Fold sides over filling. Roll up from bottom to enclose filling. Cut in half diagonally. Makes 4 wraps.

1 wrap: 626 Calories; 28.1 g Total Fat (14.1 g Mono, 8.8 g Poly, 3.3 g Sat); 123 mg Cholesterol; 60 g Carbohydrate; 2 g Fibre; 32 g Protein; 589 mg Sodium

tortilla wraps

Cook up a double batch of the first four ingredients and freeze half for another busy night. Make more tortillas or add the beef to tomato sauce for a fast pasta.

Cooking oil	1 tsp.	5 mL
Finely chopped onion	1 1/4 cups	300 mL
Garlic cloves, minced	2	2
Lean ground beef	1 1/2 lbs.	680 g
Can of red kidney beans, rinsed, drained and chopped	14 oz.	398 mL
Prepared beef broth	2/3 cup	150 mL
Water	1/2 cup	125 mL
Tomato paste (see Tip, page 64)	1/4 cup	60 mL
Envelope of taco seasoning mix	1 1/4 oz.	35 g
Chopped fresh oregano	1 tbsp.	15 mL
Tomato (or spinach) flour tortillas (9 inch, 22 cm, diameter)	6	6
Chopped fresh cilantro or parsley	1/3 cup	75 mL
Grated medium Cheddar cheese	1 cup	250 mL

Sprigs of fresh cilantro (or parsley), for garnish

Heat cooking oil in large frying pan on medium-high. Add onion and garlic. Cook for about 5 to 10 minutes, stirring often, until onion is softened.

Add beef. Scramble-fry for about 5 minutes until no longer pink. Drain. Return to same pan.

Add beans. Stir. Add next 5 ingredients. Stir. Simmer, uncovered, for 10 minutes until boiling and thickened.

Spoon about 2/3 cup (150 mL) beef mixture along centre of each tortilla. Sprinkle 2 1/2 tsp. (12 mL) cilantro over beef mixture. Roll up tightly. Arrange, seam-side down, on greased baking sheet. Sprinkle with cheese. Bake in 350°F (175°C) oven for about 15 minutes until cheese is melted and tortillas are golden.

Garnish with cilantro sprigs. Makes 6 wraps.

1 wrap: 539 Calories; 19.2 g Total Fat (5.3 g Mono, 0.8 g Poly, 7.4 g Sat); 103 mg Cholesterol; 44 g Carbohydrate; 7 g Fibre; 46 g Protein; 1034 mg Sodium

pesto chicken wraps

A store-bought roasted chicken makes this recipe quicker and easier. And if you don't have a two-sided electric grill, bake at 425°F (220°C) for about 10 minutes until crisp.

Fresh asparagus spears, trimmed of tough ends	6	6
Sun-dried tomato pesto	1/3 cup	75 mL
Light mayonnaise	2 tbsp.	30 mL
Flour tortillas (9 inch, 22 cm, diameter)	2	2
Chopped cooked chicken	2 cups	500 mL
Coarsely chopped roasted red peppers	1/2 cup	125 mL
Thinly sliced fresh white mushrooms	1/2 cup	125 mL

Pour water into large frying pan until about 1 inch (2.5 cm) deep. Bring to a boil. Reduce heat to medium. Add asparagus. Boil gently, covered, for about 2 minutes until tender-crisp. Drain well.

Combine pesto and mayonnaise in small bowl. Spread over tortillas.

Layer remaining 3 ingredients and asparagus along centre of tortillas. Fold sides over filling. Roll up from bottom to enclose filling. Preheat two-sided electric grill for 5 minutes. Place wraps on greased grill. Close lid. Cook for about 5 minutes until crisp and browned. Cut in half diagonally. Serves 4.

1 serving: 340 Calories; 14.5 g Total Fat (4.1 g Mono, 2.6 g Poly, 3.3 g Sat); 77 mg Cholesterol; 20 g Carbohydrate; 1 g Fibre; 29 g Protein; 813 mg Sodium

slow-cooker fajitas

Once you've turned the slow cooker off, gather the rest of the ingredients on the counter and have guests or family members assemble their own wraps. Make sure to have lots of napkins on hand.

Beef sirloin tip steak, cut into thin strips	1 1/2 lbs.	680 g
Thickly sliced fresh white mushrooms	2 cups	500 mL
Medium red pepper, cut into 1/2 inch (12 mm) strips	1	1
Medium yellow pepper, cut into 1/2 inch (12 mm) strips	1	1
Large onion, cut lengthwise into 8 wedges	1	1
Finely chopped pickled jalapeño peppers, drained (optional)	1 tbsp.	15 mL
Water	1/4 cup	60 mL
Envelope of fajita seasoning mix	1 oz.	28 g
Flour tortillas (7 1/2 inch, 19 cm, diameter)	10	10
Medium avocado, diced	1	1
Lemon juice	2 tsp.	10 mL
Light sour cream	2/3 cup	150 mL
Grated jalapeño Monterey Jack cheese	2/3 cup	150 mL
Medium tomato, diced	1	1
Shredded lettuce, lightly packed	1 cup	250 mL

Layer first 6 ingredients, in order given, in 3 1/2 to 4 quart (3.5 to 4 L) slow cooker.

Combine water and seasoning mix in small bowl. Add to slow cooker. Cook, covered, on Low for 5 to 6 hours or on High for 2 1/2 to 3 hours until beef is tender.

Drain beef and vegetables. Spoon about 1/2 cup (125 mL) beef mixture down centre of each tortilla.

Combine avocado and lemon juice in small bowl. Spoon avocado mixture over beef.

Layer remaining 4 ingredients, in order given, over avocado. Fold bottom over filling. Fold in sides, leaving top open. Makes 10 fajitas.

1 fajita: 358 Calories; 16.5 g Total Fat (4.8 g Mono, 1.1 g Poly, 5.5 g Sat); 56 mg Cholesterol; 32 g Carbohydrate; 3 g Fibre; 22 g Protein; 698 mg Sodium

asian vegetable wraps

Hoisin sauce is the Chinese equivalent of North America's barbecue sauce. It's delicious as a glaze for meat and poultry, but its blend of sweet, salty and sour flavours also works well in a stir-fry or as a dip.

Sesame (or cooking) oil	1 tsp.	5 mL
Thinly sliced red onion	1 cup	250 mL
Garlic cloves, minced (or 1/2 tsp., 2 mL, powder)	2	2
Thinly sliced red pepper	1 cup	250 mL
Thinly sliced yellow pepper	1 cup	250 mL
Can of shoestring-style bamboo shoots, drained	8 oz.	227 mL
Thinly sliced fresh shiitake mushrooms	1/2 cup	125 mL
Hoisin sauce	2 tsp.	10 mL
Soy sauce	1 tsp.	5 mL
Salt	1/2 tsp.	2 mL
Pepper	1/4 tsp.	1 mL
Fresh bean sprouts	2 cups	500 mL
Hoisin sauce	2 tbsp.	30 mL
Flour tortillas (9 inch, 22 cm, diameter)	4	4

Heat sesame oil in large frying pan on medium. Add onion and garlic. Cook for 5 to 10 minutes, stirring often, until onion is softened.

Add next 8 ingredients. Cook for 3 to 5 minutes, stirring occasionally, until peppers are tender-crisp.

Add bean sprouts. Heat and stir for 1 to 2 minutes until bean sprouts start to wilt.

Spread second amount of hoisin sauce over tortillas. Cut tortillas in half. Spoon vegetable mixture along tortilla halves. Fold bottom ends over filling. Fold in sides, leaving top ends open. Makes 8 wraps. Serves 4.

1 serving: 265 Calories; 6.2 g Total Fat (0.6 g Mono, 1.0 g Poly, 1.4 g Sat); trace Cholesterol; 48 g Carbohydrate; 5 g Fibre; 9 g Protein; 850 mg Sodium

shanghai wraps

If you like, sprinkle on some toasted sesame seeds (see page 64) before wrapping for extra Asian flair.

Large egg, fork-beaten	1	1
Lean ground pork	1 lb.	454 g
Fine dry bread crumbs	1/2 cup	125 mL
Finely chopped celery	1/4 cup	60 mL
Thinly sliced green onion	1/4 cup	60 mL
Low-sodium soy sauce	2 tbsp.	30 mL
Finely grated ginger root	2 tsp.	10 mL
Garlic cloves, minced	2	2
Cayenne pepper	1/4 tsp.	1 mL
Salt	1/8 tsp.	0.5 mL
Pepper, sprinkle		
Can of whole baby corn, drained	14 oz.	398 mL
Flour tortillas (9 inch, 22 cm, diameter)	6	6
Hoisin sauce	2 tbsp.	30 mL
Chopped fresh bean sprouts	1 cup	250 mL
Grated carrot	1/3 cup	75 mL
Green onions, thinly sliced lengthwise	2	2

Preheat electric grill for 5 minutes or gas barbecue to high. Combine first 11 ingredients in medium bowl. Divide into 6 equal portions. Form each portion into flattened patty or sausage shape. Place on greased grill. Close lid. Cook for about 12 minutes, turning frequently, until no longer pink inside. Transfer to plate.

Cook baby corn on hot grill, turning several times, until heated through and slightly browned.

With fingers, sprinkle water over tortillas. Stack. Wrap with foil. Place on grill. Close lid. Heat for about 6 minutes, turning once, until warmed.

Spread about 1 tsp. (5 mL) hoisin sauce along centre of each tortilla. Layer 1 pork portion and about 3 baby corn over sauce.

Sprinkle remaining 3 ingredients over baby corn. Fold sides over filling. Roll up from bottom to enclose. Cut in half to serve. Makes 6 wraps.

1 wrap: 513 Calories; 22.5 g Total Fat (7.6 g Mono, 2.0 g Poly, 6.2 g Sat); 106 mg Cholesterol; 50 g Carbohydrate; 3 g Fibre; 30 g Protein; 949 mg Sodium

chard rolls

Swiss chard is a member of the beet family. New shoots are a great addition to any salad, while more mature leaves are frequently steamed or, as in this case, stuffed. The cooked rolls can be frozen in a single layer and then transferred to a freezer container.

Water	16 cups	4 L
Large Swiss (or ruby) chard leaves	10	10
Cooking oil	1 tbsp.	15 mL
Chopped onion	1 cup	250 mL
Finely chopped fresh jalapeño pepper (see Tip, page 64)	1	1
Water	2 cups	500 mL
Chopped sun-dried tomato	1/4 cup	60 mL
Vegetable (or chicken) bouillon powder	2 tbsp.	30 mL
Coarsely ground pepper	1/4 tsp.	1 mL
Medium- (or long-) grain brown rice	3/4 cup	175 mL
Water	2/3 cup	150 mL

Pour first amount of water into large pot or Dutch oven. Bring to a boil. Cut chard leaves in half lengthwise. Remove central ribs. Stack leaves. Gently push, all at once, into boiling water. Boil for about 10 seconds until soft. Drain. Let stand until cool. Restack leaves. Set aside.

Heat cooking oil in medium saucepan on medium. Add onion and jalapeño pepper. Cook for 5 to 10 minutes, stirring often, until onion is softened.

Add next 4 ingredients. Bring to a boil. Add rice. Stir. Reduce heat to low. Cover. Simmer for about 50 minutes, without stirring, until liquid is absorbed and rice is tender. Let stand until cool enough to handle. Place 1 1/2 tbsp. (25 mL) rice mixture on each chard leaf half. Fold sides over filling. Roll up tightly from bottom to enclose. Arrange in single layer in greased 2 quart (2 L) shallow casserole.

Pour third amount of water over rolls. Bake, covered, in 375°F (190°C) oven for about 1 hour until chard is very tender and water is absorbed. Makes 20 rolls.

1 roll: 47 Calories; 1.1 g Total Fat (0.5 g Mono, 0.3 g Poly, 0.1 g Sat); trace Cholesterol; 8 g Carbohydrate; 1 g Fibre; 1 g Protein; 262 mg Sodium

feta and herb eggplant rolls

Because you're using Asian eggplants, you won't have to pre-salt them to reduce the bitterness. And if you don't feel like grilling the eggplants, you can bake the slices in a 375ºF (190ºC) oven for 15 to 20 minutes until lightly browned.

Asian eggplants (with peel), ends trimmed	3	3
Olive (or cooking) oil	2 tbsp.	30 mL
Salt, sprinkle		
Pepper, sprinkle		
Whole roasted red peppers, cut into 4 strips each	3	3
Crumbled feta cheese	1/2 cup	125 mL
Herb and garlic cream cheese	1/4 cup	60 mL
Chopped fresh basil	3 tbsp.	50 mL
Arugula leaves	36	36
Cocktail picks	12	12
Balsamic vinegar	2 tbsp.	30 mL

Cut eggplants lengthwise into six 1/4 inch (6 mm) slices. Discard outer slices. Brush both sides of slices with olive oil. Sprinkle with salt and pepper. Preheat electric grill for 5 minutes or gas barbecue to medium. Cook eggplant on greased grill for about 5 minutes until browned. Remove from grill. Let stand until cool.

Place 1 strip of red pepper on each eggplant slice.

Combine next 3 ingredients in small bowl. Spread over red pepper. Arrange arugula leaves over top. Roll up from bottom to enclose filling. Secure with cocktail picks. Arrange rolls, seam-side down, on plate.

Brush with vinegar. Serve at room temperature. Makes 12 rolls.

1 roll: 83 Calories; 5.6 g Total Fat (2.0 g Mono, 0.3 g Poly, 2.5 g Sat); 11 mg Cholesterol; 5 g Carbohydrate; 1 g Fibre; 2 g Protein; 222 mg Sodium

stuffed grape leaves

Warm or cold, these starters are delicious on their own or with a simple yogurt sauce. Just grate unpeeled cucumber into twice as much plain yogurt and add salt, minced garlic and chopped fresh mint to taste.

Olive (or cooking) oil	2 tsp.	10 mL
Chopped onion	1 cup	250 mL
Garlic cloves, minced	2	2
Long-grain brown rice	1 1/3 cups	325 mL
Water	2 3/4 cups	675 mL
Medium tomato, chopped	1	1
Pine nuts, toasted (see Tip, page 64) and chopped	1/4 cup	60 mL
Raisins, chopped	1/4 cup	60 mL
Chopped fresh parsley (or 1 1/2 tsp., 7 mL, flakes)	2 tbsp.	30 mL
Chicken bouillon powder	1 tsp.	5 mL
Ground cinnamon	1/4 tsp.	1 mL
Pepper, sprinkle		
Jar of grape leaves, drained	17 oz.	473 mL
Water	1/2 cup	125 mL
Lemon juice	2 tbsp.	30 mL
Olive (or cooking) oil	1 tbsp.	15 mL

Heat olive oil in large frying pan on medium. Add onion and garlic.

Cook for 5 to 10 minutes, stirring often, until onion is softened. Add rice. Cook, stirring occasionally, for about 1 minute until rice is toasted. Transfer to large saucepan.

Add next 8 ingredients. Stir. Bring to a boil. Reduce heat to medium-low. Cover. Simmer for about 40 minutes, without stirring, until liquid is absorbed and rice is tender.

Pinch stem ends off grape leaves. Using larger leaves, place about 2 rounded tablespoons (30 mL) rice mixture on underside of each leaf, near stem end. Roll up, tucking in sides to enclose filling. Use remaining leaves to line greased 3 quart (3 L) casserole. Arrange rolls, seam-side down and close together, in 2 layers.

Combine remaining 3 ingredients in small cup. Drizzle over rolls. Bake, covered, in 325°F (160°C) oven for about 1 1/2 hours until leaves are very tender and liquid is absorbed. Makes about 28 stuffed grape leaves.

1 stuffed grape leaf: 60 Calories; 2.0 g Total Fat (1.0 g Mono, 0.5 g Poly, 0.3 g Sat); trace Cholesterol; 10 g Carbohydrate; 1 g Fibre; 2 g Protein; 76 mg Sodium

leek-wrapped ginger scallops

The white part of a leek makes a perfect little wrapper to snug around a scallop. A syrupy dripping sauce adds the final touch to these low-cal, one-bite appetizers.

DIPPING SAUCE		
Soy sauce	1/2 cup	125 mL
Brown sugar, packed	2 tbsp.	30 mL

WRAPPED SCALLOPS		
Large leek (white part only), trimmed to 5 inches (12.5 cm)	1	1
Pickled ginger slices, halved	6	6
Large sea scallops	12	12
Wooden cocktail picks	12	12
Water	1/2 cup	125 mL
Soy sauce	2 tbsp.	30 mL

Dipping Sauce: Combine soy sauce and brown sugar in small saucepan on medium-low. Simmer for about 5 minutes until reduced to syrup consistency. Set aside.

Wrapped Scallops: Remove 12 leaves from centre of leek. Pour water into large saucepan until about 1 inch (2.5 cm) deep. Bring to a boil. Add leek. Boil for 1 minute to soften. Drain. Transfer to ice water for 1 minute. Drain well. Blot dry.

Place 1 ginger piece and 1 scallop on each leaf (photo 1). Secure with cocktail picks (photo 2).

Combine water and soy sauce in large frying pan on medium. Bring to a simmer. Add skewers. Cook, covered, for about 4 minutes until scallops are opaque. Using a slotted spoon, transfer to plate. Serve with Dipping Sauce. Makes 12 skewers.

1 skewer with 1 tsp. (5 mL) glaze: 30 Calories; 0.1 g Total Fat (trace Mono, trace Poly, trace Sat); 5 mg Cholesterol; 4 g Carbohydrate; trace Fibre; 3 g Protein; 590 mg Sodium

tasty lettuce wraps

Invite a friend over for a hands-on meal, or double the recipe and make this an assemble-yourself appetizer for a small crowd.

Lean ground chicken	1/2 lb.	225 g
Coarsely grated carrot	1/4 cup	60 mL
Diced celery	1/4 cup	60 mL
Diced red (or green) pepper	1/4 cup	60 mL
Green onions, sliced	2	2
Thick teriyaki basting sauce	1/3 cup	75 mL
Chili paste (sambel oelek)	1 tsp.	5 mL
Package of instant noodles	3 oz.	85 g
Iceberg lettuce leaves	12	12

Combine first 5 ingredients in 1 1/2 quart (1.5 L) microwave-safe casserole. Microwave, covered, on high (100%) for 3 minutes, stirring at halftime to break up chicken.

Add teriyaki sauce and chili paste. Mix well. Microwave, uncovered, on high (100%) for 1 minute until chicken is no longer pink.

Break up noodles. Discard seasoning packet. Add noodles to chicken mixture. Toss until coated.

To serve, spoon about 1 1/2 tbsp. (25 mL) chicken mixture along centre of each lettuce leaf. Fold sides over filling. Roll up from bottom to enclose filling. Serves 2.

1 serving: 447 Calories; 17.2 g Total Fat (0.5 g Mono, 0.6 g Poly, 0.4 g Sat); 40 mg Cholesterol; 43 g Carbohydrate; 2 g Fibre; 30 g Protein; 2040 mg Sodium

recipe index

topical tips

Chopping jalapeño peppers: Hot peppers contain capsaicin in the seeds and ribs. Removing the seeds and ribs will reduce the heat. Wear rubber gloves when handling jalapeño peppers and avoid touching your eyes. Wash your hands well afterwards.

Cutting julienne: To julienne, cut into thin strips that resemble matchsticks.

Hot-oil temperature test: A deep-fry thermometer is an easy way to ensure the oil is between 350-375ºF (170-190ºC)—the right temperature for crispy, not greasy, results. Failing that, you can insert the tip of a wooden spoon into the oil. If the oil bubbles around the tip, the temperature is correct. Or toss a bread cube into the oil. If it sizzles and browns in a minute, the oil is ready.

Tomato paste leftovers: If a recipe calls for less than an entire can of tomato paste, freeze the unopened can for 30 minutes. Open both ends and push the contents through one end. Slice off only what you need. Freeze the remaining paste in a resealable freezer bag or plastic wrap for future use.

Toasting nuts, seeds or coconut: Cooking times will vary for each ingredient, so never toast them together. For small amounts, place ingredient in an ungreased frying pan. Heat on medium for three to five minutes, stirring often, until golden. For larger amounts, spread ingredient evenly in an ungreased shallow pan. Bake in a 350ºF (175ºC) oven for five to 10 minutes, stirring or shaking often, until golden.

Nutrition Information Guidelines

Each recipe is analyzed using the Canadian Nutrient File from Health Canada, which is based on the United States Department of Agriculture (USDA) Nutrient Database.

- If more than one ingredient is listed (such as "butter or hard margarine"), or if a range is given (1 – 2 tsp., 5 – 10 mL), only the first ingredient or first amount is analyzed.

- For meat, poultry and fish, the serving size per person is based on the recommended 4 oz. (113 g) uncooked weight (without bone), which is 2 – 3 oz. (57 – 85 g) cooked weight (without bone)— approximately the size of a deck of playing cards.

- Milk used is 1% M.F. (milk fat), unless otherwise stated.

- Cooking oil used is canola oil, unless otherwise stated.

- Ingredients indicating "sprinkle," "optional" or "for garnish" are not included in the nutrition information.

- The fat in recipes and combination foods can vary greatly depending on the sources and types of fats used in each specific ingredient. For these reasons, the count of saturated, monounsaturated and polyunsaturated fats may not add up to the total fat content.